Straight Talk About...
DATE RAPE

Jessica
Wilkins

Crabtree Publishing Company
www.crabtreebooks.com

Straight
Talk About...

Developed and produced by: Plan B Book Packagers

Editorial director: Ellen Rodger

Art director: Rosie Gowsell-Pattison

Fictional Introductions: Rachel Eagen

Editor: Molly Aloian

Project coordinator: Kathy Middleton

Production coordinator: Margaret Amy Salter

Prepress technician: Margaret Amy Salter

Consultant: Susan Rodger, PhD., C. Psych.,
Psychologist and Professor Faculty of Education,
The University of Western Ontario

Photographs:
Title pg: iStockPhoto.com; p. 4: Justin Paget/
Shutterstock Inc. ; p. 6: @erics/Shutterstock Inc.; p. 8:
Jeremys78/Shutterstock Inc.; p. 9: Luca Villanova/
Shutterstock Inc.; p. 10: Tatiana Popova/Shutterstock
Inc.; p. 12: Monkey Business Images/Shutterstock Inc.;
p. 14: Justin Paget/Shutterstock Inc.; p. 15: Vladimir
Wrangel/Shutterstock Inc.; p. 17: Monkey Business
Images/Shutterstock Inc.; p. 18: iStockPhoto.com; p. 19:
iofoto/Shutterstock Inc.; p. 20: Justin Paget/Shutterstock
Inc.; p. 21: Claus Mikosch/Shutterstock Inc.; p. 22: Roz
Design/Shutterstock Inc.; p. 24: iStockPhoto.com; p. 25:
iStockPhoto.com; p. 26: Wallenrock/Shutterstock Inc.;
p. 27: Supri Suharjoto/Shutterstock Inc.; p. 28:
iStockPhoto.com; p. 29: iStockPhoto.com; p. 32:
Adam J. Sablich/Shutterstock Inc.; p. 33: Roxana
Gonzalez/Shutterstock Inc.; p. 34: (left) Bogdan
Ionescu/Shutterstock Inc., (right) Vlue/Shutterstock
Inc.; p. 36: iStockPhoto.com; p. 38: (right)
iStockPhoto.com, (left) Justin Paget/Shutterstock Inc.

Library and Archives Canada Cataloguing in Publication

Wilkins, Jessica
    Date rape / Jessica Wilkins.

(Straight talk about--)
Includes index.
Issued also in an electronic format.
ISBN 978-0-7787-2128-4 (bound).--ISBN 978-0-7787-2135-2 (pbk.)

    1. Date rape--Juvenile literature. I. Title.
II. Series: Straight talk about-- (St. Catharines, Ont.)

HQ801.83.W54 2010   j362.883   C2010-902765-5

Library of Congress Cataloging-in-Publication Data

Wilkins, Jessica.
    Date rape / Jessica Wilkins.
      p. cm. -- (Straight talk about--)
    Includes index.
    ISBN 978-0-7787-2135-2 (pbk. : alk. paper) --
    ISBN 978-0-7787-2128-4 (reinforced library binding : alk. paper)
    -- ISBN 978-1-4271-9541-8 (electronic (pdf))
    1. Date rape--Juvenile literature. 2. Dating violence--Juvenile
literature. 3. Date rape--Prevention--Juvenile literature.
4. Dating violence--Prevention--Juvenile literature. I. Title.
II. Series.

HQ801.83.W57 2011
362.883--dc22
                                      2010016397

Crabtree Publishing Company

www.crabtreebooks.com   1-800-387-7650

Printed in China/082010/AP20100512

Published in Canada
Crabtree Publishing
616 Welland Ave.
St. Catharines, ON
L2M 5V6

Published in the United States
Crabtree Publishing
PMB 59051
350 Fifth Avenue, 59th Floor
New York, NY 10118

Published in the United Kingdom
Crabtree Publishing
Maritime House
Basin Road North, Hove
BN41 1WR

Published in Australia
Crabtree Publishing
386 Mt. Alexander Rd.
Ascot Vale (Melbourne)
VIC 3032

CONTENTS

"Race you?" Max blew his hair out of his eyes and looked at Basima. His freckles were starting to show through. By the end of the summer, he'd be covered.

Basima adjusted her headscarf. "Sure, but you know I always win."

Max took off ahead of her. Cheater. But Basima knew she could beat him. She'd grown at least two inches since last summer.

She caught up to him halfway through the field. "Gotcha!" she yelled as her fingers grazed his t-shirt. Suddenly, she was tripping, falling. She landed hard on the ground, hearing a loud snap in her wrist and the spread of hot pain searing up her arm. She tasted grass and dirt.

"My wrist," Basima gasped. She turned to look up. Max was standing over her, staring at her.

Max knelt down in front of her. "You tripped," he said.

"You did it on purpose," she cried. "I think I broke it." Her arm was already starting to swell. "Help me, Max."

Max was staring at Basima. The look in his eyes made her feel very afraid.

"Max, I need to go home." She was starting to cry.

"No, you don't." Max put his hand on Basima's shoulder. He pushed her, lightly.

"Don't, Max."

"Shut up." Now he was forcing. Pushing. Pressing. She tried to push him off but her wrist wouldn't work. And he was so strong. Too strong.

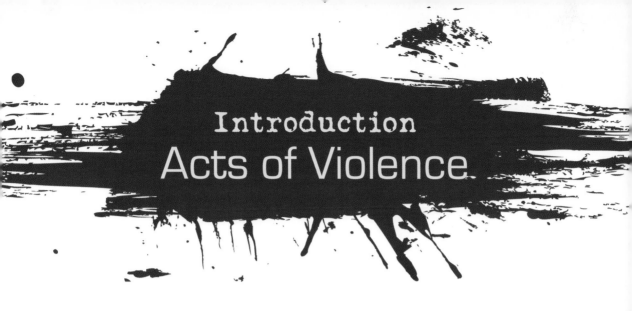

Introduction
Acts of Violence

Dating violence and date rape are acts of power and control. They can include forced sexual intercourse, or other things that make you feel uncomfortable or unsafe, like unwanted attention, jokes, mean comments, harrassment, or touching that is not okay with you.

In this book, you will learn about date rape and why it's important to speak out if it ever happens to you, a family member, or a friend. You will also learn the difference between a healthy relationship and an unhealthy relationship, how to set boundaries, and ways you can protect yourself.

"If you love a person, it doesn't mean you have to sleep with them. A lot of times guys will try to tell you you have to, or if you don't they say that you did anyway. Or they make comments about your body or jokes. That's not right. It's disrespectful."
Samira, aged 15.

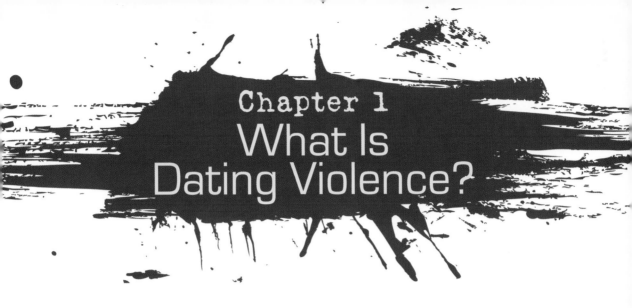

Chapter 1
What Is Dating Violence?

Have you ever been threatened, **humiliated**, or called hurtful names by a boyfriend or girlfriend, but ignored it because you felt it wasn't that bad, or loved the person, or were afraid that he or she might hurt you? Threats, **intimidation**, and name-calling are a form of dating violence. Dating violence is a pattern of behavior where one person threatens, or actually uses, physical, sexual, **verbal**, or emotional abuse against a dating partner.

Dating violence can happen once or many times in a relationship. A person may experience one type of violence, such as emotional abuse, or a combination of many types of abuse. Date rape, or sexual assault, is another form of dating violence.

Dating violence is common. In the United States, one in three adolescent girls experiences physical, emotional, or verbal abuse from a dating partner. This statistic is higher than other types of violence that affect youth, including gun violence.

All forms of dating violence are wrong and some are also against the law.

Someone You Know

Dating violence, or dating abuse, is the term used to describe violence that occurs within a social or **intimate** relationship between two people. Research shows that violence against girls happens most often with someone that they know. It can be a person they are dating or even an acquaintance. An acquaintance is anyone who is known to you, or who is not a stranger. Some examples include a person you meet at a party, a friend of a friend, a neighbor, or someone from your class or school. Dating violence can also happen between people of the same sex. Gay, lesbian, bisexual, **transgendered**, and **questioning** youths are just as likely to experience dating violence and date rape, as **heterosexual** youths. They may also be less likely to report dating violence out of fear they they will not be taken seriously or will be **harassed** by others.

Physical Abuse

Dating violence is an attempt to control another person through physical, emotional, or sexual abuse. Physical abuse is any intentional, unwanted contact from a date, boyfriend, or girlfriend. It includes actions such as scratching, punching, biting, kicking, throwing something at you, pulling hair, choking, using a weapon, and shoving. A sharp shove into a wall isn't just horsing around—it is physical abuse.

8

A Way with Words

Emotional abuse is anything a person does that makes their partner feel scared, lowers their self-confidence, controls them, or makes them feel **inferior**. Some examples of emotional abuse are: calling a boyfriend or girlfriend names, wanting to know where a partner is at all times, constant criticism, or spreading gossip or spiteful rumors. Posting intimate or nasty things about a date on a Facebook page is emotionally abusive. Threatening to do harm to yourself to prevent a breakup, or being extremely jealous or possessive is also abusive.

Pressure to Have Sex

Have you ever felt pressured to have sex when you didn't want to? Like physical and emotional abuse, sexual abuse is considered an act of power and not of love. Sexual abuse is any unwanted sexual activity. It can be rape, or sexual assault. It can also be **coercion** or harrassment. Making a partner have sex with you by lying, or **manipulating** them, is abusive. Not stopping when someone says no, or forcing someone to go further than they want to is sexual assault. It is also a crime.

It's Not your Fault

Dating violence can happen anywhere—in a car, at a party, at school, or in your home. Violence also doesn't know skin color, sexual orientation, or class. This means that dating violence can happen to anyone at anytime, no matter who they are or what they look like.

Sometimes people think that they cause the violence because of something they said or did. Survivors of dating violence, including date rape, should never be blamed for what they have experienced. You should never feel guilty if someone uses physical, sexual, or verbal violence to try to control you, humiliate you, or put you down. No matter what the circumstances, dating violence is never the victim's fault.

Phone Threats

Cell phones can be a great way to keep in touch with friends and family, but they can also be a tool for abusers to keep track of boyfriends and girlfriends, and can contribute to dating violence. Sending threatening text messages, and demanding to know where a girlfriend or boyfriend is all the time, is abusive behavior. Calling repeatedly, or asking a boyfriend or girlfriend to check in many times an hour or day, is controlling, not caring. Controlling behavior is abusive because it makes it hard to be yourself in a relationship. It can also lead to more abuse, including physical violence.

Where are you?!

Internet Gossip and Lies

Most adolescents use computers and the Internet to chat to friends and family, do research for school, and learn about interesting things. But computers are also sometimes used as a tool for dating violence. Sending threatening emails, or writing nasty things and spreading gossip about a partner or former partner on Internet **forums**, such as networking Web sites or blogs, is abusive and wrong.

Relationship Roller Coaster

Dating can be really complicated. We get information about relationships from many different places including our families, friends, television, magazines, and books. Sometimes the information is good and sometime it is just wrong. It may even feel like some amount of violence happens in all relationships. If a friend tells you that all boys push their girlfriends around, you're getting bad advice. Healthy, loving relationships come with ups and downs, disagreements, and sometimes hurt feelings. They do not include threats and violent actions. Ever.

When you are dating, the most important thing to remember is that everyone has the right to a relationship free from violence or fear, and you do not have to endure any form of violence. Relationships are never perfect, and maintaining one that works for you may take some work for both partners. Healthy relationships are built on mutual honesty, respect, and open communication. This means you should feel free to talk to your partner about what is important to you without fear. You should also feel loved and respected for the person you are.

"I think a person shouldn't try to change you to be someone else. They should like you for who you are."
Evan, aged 14.

Chapter 2
Healthy Relationships

Healthy relationships are built on respect, communication, and trust. Healthy communication means that both partners in a relationship can talk openly and honestly with one another. This means that you feel comfortable and safe enough to express your thoughts and feelings about an issue. It also means being open to hearing your partner's **perspective** on a situation. Communicating in a healthy way means getting to say your piece and then allowing your partner to express his or her opinions without forcing yours just to win an argument.

Safety and Equality

A healthy relationship should feel safe and make you feel like you are an equal partner. What does safety feel like? Safety will feel different for everyone, but generally, it should mean that you are not fearful of your partner, that you feel like you can speak your mind, and trust them to respect what you say.

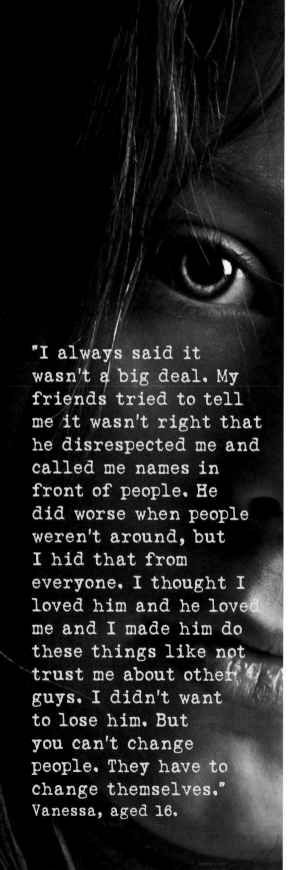

"I always said it wasn't a big deal. My friends tried to tell me it wasn't right that he disrespected me and called me names in front of people. He did worse when people weren't around, but I hid that from everyone. I thought I loved him and he loved me and I made him do these things like not trust me about other guys. I didn't want to lose him. But you can't change people. They have to change themselves."
Vanessa, aged 16.

Me Time

Being in a healthy relationship does not mean that you need to be happy all the time. All relationships have arguments and disagreements. It is how you choose to resolve your disagreements that really counts. Another important aspect of healthy relationships is balance. This means balancing your needs with your boyfriend's or girlfriend's, and feeling like you are getting out of it what you are putting into it. It also means a balance between your relationship and other parts of your life, such as friends, family, and school. When you really like someone, it is natural to feel like you would like to spend as much time together as possible. But it is important to make time for all the relationships in your life. Those relationships shape who you are as a person.

Communication and Respect

How do we build a healthy relationship with a boyfriend or girlfriend? The first step is to make sure that both you and your partner are clear about what you want and expect out of the relationship. This means communicating. Support your partner and feel free to let your partner know when you need a little extra support, too. Respect and maintain each other's "space." Just because you are in a relationship doesn't mean you need to be together all the time or know everything about each other. Speak up when something is bothering you (there's that communication stuff again). Talk to your boyfriend or girlfriend when you feel unhappy and work together toward **compromises** if you have disagreements.

Rights and Responsibilities

As a partner in a healthy relationship, you have certain rights and responsibilities. This means that you can expect things from your boyfriend or girlfriend, and in turn, they can expect the same things from you.

Relationships are not always easy, but they should not make you feel horrible about yourself.

Dating Rights

I have the right to say yes or no to any activity without feeling guilty.

I have the right to suggest doing an activity together.

I have the right to speak my mind and talk about things that are important to me.

I have the right to be myself in my relationship.

I have the right to change a relationship if my feelings change.

If my relationship ends, I have the right to not blame myself.

I have the right to have my values and beliefs respected.

I have the right to have friends and other relationships outside of my dating partner.

I have the right to refuse any sexual activity (from hugging and kissing to oral sex or intercourse) at ANY TIME for ANY REASON, and my partner may do the same. I am responsible for my words and actions within my relationship.

I must communicate using my words, not fists.

I am responsible for listening to what my partner has to say.

Your Own Support Group

Friends can give really great advice and give us support when we are in relationships. It is important to remember though, that you are in charge of your thoughts, feelings, and actions with your boyfriend or girlfriend. In a relationship, you and your partner are the most important people. Friends may give you advice about what to do in a relationship, but at the end of the day, you make the decisions.

Having a friend or group of friends to turn to can be really helpful. They can be a source of strength in hard times.

Chapter 3
Power and Control

Dating can be difficult, especially when you are new to it. It is hard to know how to act. It can also be hard to know your rights and responsibilities. Is it okay to say no to a date? (Yes, it is most definitely okay.) Should you let a boyfriend or girlfriend boss you around just to make them happy? (No, you should not!)

How do you know you are in a relationship that is not healthy? Dating violence is any form of threatening or intimidating behavior against an intimate partner, whether that is physical, verbal, emotional, or sexual. Dating violence can happen once, or it can happen many times. You can experience dating violence with a boyfriend or girlfriend, a friend, or an acquaintance. It can happen to anyone from any race, religion, class, or sexual orientation. Often, it is hidden because a victim might feel ashamed or embarrassed.

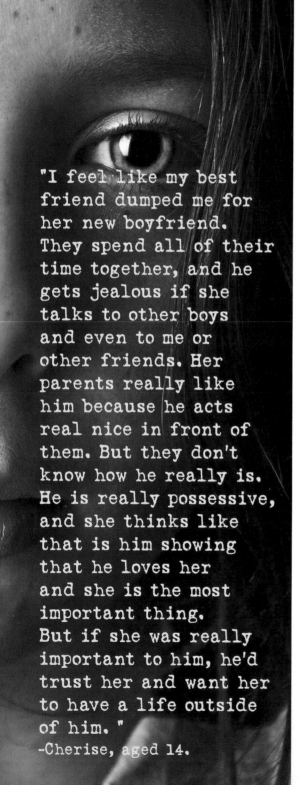

"I feel like my best friend dumped me for her new boyfriend. They spend all of their time together, and he gets jealous if she talks to other boys and even to me or other friends. Her parents really like him because he acts real nice in front of them. But they don't know how he really is. He is really possessive, and she thinks like that is him showing that he loves her and she is the most important thing. But if she was really important to him, he'd trust her and want her to have a life outside of him."
-Cherise, aged 14.

Just Young Love?

Psychologists call dating violence "intimate partner violence" because it involves someone you know. That someone can be a casual dating partner, a boyfriend or girlfriend, a friend, someone you just met, or someone you are having sex with.

Dating violence is often minimized, or underestimated. Some people, including those closest to you such as friends or parents, might say a boyfriend or girlfriend who demands you spend all your time with them is just "showing their love." You may hear the expressions "oh, that's young love" or "it was just a push" to excuse an act of violence as an act of romantic love. These explanations are misleading. Nobody should feel pressured into accepting manipulative, controlling, or violent behavior as normal or acceptable.

It's About Power

Dating violence isn't about love. It is about power. What you might not know is that a lot of dating violence isn't just about hitting. It's about controlling a date or partner and having power over them. A person might exert control over a date by using their **social status**, or threats and intimidation to get their date to do what they want. They might be really well liked, or the coolest kid in school, but that does not give them the right to tell you what to do, or control or manipulate you.

Dating violence is about one person thinking that they have the right to have power over someone else—that they have the right to control them. Sometimes you might even experience dating violence and not even realize it because we assume that violence is just about hitting. It's not. It's about power. If your date or partner treats you like a servant, doesn't let you hang out with your friends, or threatens to tell other people private stuff about you, they are using power to control you. That is wrong, and it is abuse.

Dating shouldn't be an emotional tug of war.

Don't Blame Yourself

Someone who is being abused by a partner might feel ashamed, blame themselves, or wish that their partner would change. Some may feel **anxious**, fearful, or extremely sad. Have you ever heard that jealousy or even physical abuse is romantic? It's not. When a person is jealous, that is their issue. That is how they feel, and they need to find a way to deal with their feelings of doubt and insecurity. You don't have to feel responsible for how someone else feels or acts. It is not your fault that they feel jealous or act violently.

Are You Abusive?

What we say and the way we act affects everyone around us. If you yell or use violent behavior, you will frighten those around you. If you call your date stupid, they will believe that is what you think about them, and worse, they may even believe it about themselves. Many young people see violence all around them. It is a part of our culture. It is in music, in movies, on television, and in video games. The media tells us that using physical violence and threats get us what we want in life. Not only are those messages untrue—using violence will not get you what you want, but it will get you a trip to jail—they are dangerous.

Deal with It

Do you feel jealous when your date talks to other girls or guys? Have you ever used physical force or threats to get a date to obey you or to do exactly what you want? You might feel like you need to do these things or you won't feel respected or strong. But respect does not come with using force. Respect only comes with trust and when you value and support a partner or date. You do not have the right to control what your date or partner does. Your date is their own person and has the right to say and do what they want. If you respect their beliefs, thoughts, and wishes, they will respect yours in return. And that feels better than control.

If you have threatened or used physical force, called a date hurtful names to humiliate them, or forced someone to have sex when she or he did not want to, you have acted in an abusive way. Using violence is something a person chooses to do. There are no excuses for your words or actions. Don't try to blame someone else. "She just made me so angry," is no excuse for violence. These are your feelings, and you must learn to deal with them in ways that are not violent or controlling. If you have abused a date, take responsibility by getting help. This means talking to a counselor, a teacher, or someone who understands healthy relationships. There are programs that can teach you how to stop your abusive behavior. This change might be hard, but those who really want to change can be successful.

Chapter 4
Sexual Assault

You are probably familiar with the term "date rape." Date rape is a sexual assault that happens between two partners who know each other. Sexual assault is any unwanted sexual activity that occurs without your consent. This includes inappropriate or unwanted touching, and vaginal, anal, or oral rape, or assault. Consent means that you voluntarily say "yes" to engage in an activity. You can indicate "no" to your partner through your words, by saying "no" or "stop" or "don't," or through your actions, such as pushing your partner away or trying to leave.

"No," doesn't have to be said; it can be implied through actions.

Date Rape Drugs

Sometimes drugs and alcohol are used in date rapes. Alcohol can make you drowsy and unable to fend off an assault. Date rape drugs are slipped into drinks without your knowledge. The drugs can make you feel physically weak or confused so that you can't refuse or defend yourself against an attack. If you are raped while someone has given you drugs, you might not remember what happened. Some common date rape drugs are rohypnol, often called "forget pills," "roofies," or "lunch money," GHB, which is nicknamed "cherry meth," or "easy lay," and ketamine, sometimes called "kit kat," "psychadelic heroin," or "Special K." Rohypnol and GHB are not legal in the United States. Using date rape drugs during a sexual assault carries harsh penalties.

Voluntary Consent

Consent needs to be voluntary. Consent is not legally given if: someone else says yes for you; if you change your mind; if you say yes only because you are scared that you might get hurt; or if you say yes when you have had too much alcohol to drink or have been drugged. Each new sexual activity needs to be okay with both partners, which means that just because you say yes to oral sex, it does not mean you have said yes to intercourse. It also means that you can change your mind at any time. Just because you say yes to kissing and touching, doesn't mean you have to go further.

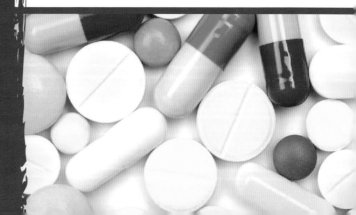

Everyone Is Vulnerable

Sexual assault can occur in many different situations, to all types of people. Sexual assault can happen to anyone, including both men and women. Girls can sexually assault other girls, and boys can assault boys. Sexual assault can happen with a friend, an acquaintance or someone you know, someone you are casually dating, or someone you are in a relationship with. Being in a relationship or having had sex with someone before do not mean it is okay to be forced into sex.

When some people feel scared for their life, or if they have been threatened, they may freeze or feel unable to fight back. This can happen when someone is sexually assaulted. They may be so frightened they freeze, or they may hope that if they don't fight back it will be over sooner.

Rape can happen between couples who have been together for a long time.

Violence and Power

It may sound odd, but sexual assault is about power, not sex. Sexual assault does NOT happen because one person got so **aroused** that they could not control themselves when the other person said "no." Sexual assault is a chosen act of violence against a chosen victim. Sexual assault is never the victim's fault. EVER.

"I never reported my rape. I kept it a secret for years because I thought it was my fault for leading him on. It was a friend. Or a so-called friend. Now I know that rape isn't just someone being too passionate and losing control. It took me a long time to understand that it wasn't me who made him do this. I am still dealing with what happened. It just makes me feel creepy to know that he might have done it to others too."
Carol, adult survivor of sexual assault.

"I feel so ashamed"

There are many ways that someone might react to experiencing sexual assault, and everyone will be different. There is no right or wrong way to feel after a sexual assault. One person might feel numb and fearful. Another might feel anxious or ashamed. They might feel that it was their fault. Sometimes people feel guilty because they did not physically fight off their attacker during the sexual assault. Other reactions might include having difficulty concentrating, constantly thinking about the attack, or having images and memories pop into your mind when you don't want them to. Survivors might have trouble sleeping or eating, or they might sleep and eat more than usual.

Some survivors may continue to feel upset for a long time following an attack, others might seem okay at first and then have trouble later. They might have health problems, such as stomachaches, headaches, or trouble sleeping.

Sexual assault is **traumatic**. It isn't something you "get over," but you can learn to cope with the feelings and emotions that affect you afterward.

29

By Force

Statistics show that about one in five high school girls has been sexually abused by a dating partner. This doesn't necessarily mean that they have been vaginally raped. Sometimes the abuse includes forced oral sex or other acts. Girls who date older boys are more likely to be sexually assaulted, manipulated, or pressured into sex. Sometimes adolescents believe that it is not sexual assault if someone is coerced into having sex or that if it isn't rape it isn't serious. But no one should feel forced or pressured into something they don't want to do. Girls also shouldn't feel they have to be sexually active to be popular. Not everybody is "doing it." The bottom line is, sexual assault is wrong and against the law.

Same-sex Assault

Lesbian, gay, bisexual, transgendered, and questioning (LGBTQ) youth are often reluctant to report assaults by dating partners. Because they are harassed often every day just for being gay, it makes them afraid to seek help for something a date did to them. They may think the police won't believe them or their families will reject them. In some cases, this is true. Statistics show that up to 50 percent of people who identify as LGBTQ will experience abuse at the hands of an intimate partner. But there is support for victims of same-sex assault. Many LGBTQ groups for adults offer services to youth and have a good understanding of the worries and roadblocks that LGBTQ youth face.

Sexual Assault Safety and Survival

If you have been sexually assaulted, go to a safe place away from your attacker as quickly as possible. Once you are in a safe place, you can think about what kind of support you need most. There are a number of different support options that you can access if you feel like they are right for you. Remember that you have options, and you are in charge of what happens next:

1. You may want to talk to a friend, family member, or someone you trust. Many people feel fearful, shocked, ashamed, and guilty after they survive a sexual assault. Having someone to talk to, and to support you can help make a difference. It might also be helpful to speak with a professional such as a psychologist or counselor, or with your local rape crisis center.

2. You should go to a hospital emergency room. It is important to be checked medically after a sexual assault. You don't have to go to the hospital alone. If you don't have anyone to go with you, ask someone from a rape crisis center to come with you. They are trained to be supportive and act in your best interest. At the hospital, a doctor will do a rape kit, taking samples of hair, fibers, saliva, and semen. They will also screen you for sexually transmitted infections (STI's) and treat you for pregnancy or injuries.

3. Report what happened to the police. The police can help protect you from your attacker or help you press charges. If you are anxious about speaking with the police, ask a friend or family member to speak with you. Rape crisis centers also have people who can go with you so you are not alone.

Popular culture shows sexualized images of women. Sexualized means to make sexual or give a role. This encourages us to think a woman's value comes from their sex appeal or behavior and not from other characteristics.

Chapter 5
Media Aware

We get a lot of information about relationships from what we see on television, on music videos, in magazines, and in movies. All of these popular media sources give suggestions about what it means to be male or female. Often, the ideal woman is portrayed as **passive** and supportive while men are shown as aggressive and powerful. These images affect the way we think about relationships and can actually work against us.

If men always need to be powerful and strong, and women always need to be supportive and passive, how can we have an equal, trusting relationship? Quite simply, the media images don't work. They show us one thing, and we are told to be another. This can be confusing.

In relationships of equality, men can be supportive without being controlling.

"At first it was flattering, all the attention. He was so cute and popular and he was my everything. He would get angry for no reason and call me names or come after me. The last time, he beat me up at a friend's house. I had to go to the hospital. When I told my parents and got a restraining order, he couldn't go back to our school. Some girls blamed me. They asked how I could do this to him? Force him to go to another school. But I was the one who got beat up, and I was the one who was scared. It was like he was excused or congratulated for what he did."
Amy, aged 16.

Booty-licious?

We've all seen music videos where women's bodies are portrayed as objects for men to **ogle**. In some videos and other media representations, women are shown as powerful when they are sexy. They are "empowered" to show their perfect bodies and booties. Men are depicted as powerful when they treat women as disposable playthings. How does this reflect healthy relationships?

Showing your feelings through anger and violence is wrong.

Mixed Messages

Popular culture tells us how young women and men should act, and it sends mixed messages about relationships. Many movie, book, or television relationships, especially those that show adolescents or teen relationships, are unequal. One person has more power than the other. One person makes more decisions or decides how the other person should act.

In popular media, romantic love is portrayed as all-consuming. Couples spend all of their time together. They take on roles where one partner is strong and protective and the other is nurturing and accepting. These are called **gender roles**. Gender roles are used to describe the way society expects people of a certain gender (male, female, somewhere in between, or neither) to behave. Sometimes, the partners act in a jealous or controlling way, which implies that they are being protective of their partner. When we see relationships portrayed this way, it **normalizes** relationship inequality. This means that if it looks like every relationship is one of inequality, we start to think that maybe that is the way it should be.

Society often expects men to be strong and women to be weak, but we know that both can be strong.

Chapter 6
Seeking Help

Sometimes people who experience dating violence can feel ashamed and guilty, and they might not want to tell anyone about what they are going through. They might worry, "what if no one believes me?" Or they might believe they caused the abuse through their actions or behavior.

It may be difficult for adolescents to leave abusive relationships. They may fear **reprisals**, or an act of retaliation, such as violence or threats of violence. It may even be hard for them to accept that everyone has the right to a relationship that is safe.

No one deserves to be hurt or left to cope with their feelings alone. It can be scary to think or talk about abuse you have experienced. Talking to a safe person that you can trust can help you to feel better and can help you to take the steps you need to live free from violence. Keeping the secret of abuse can keep you away from people who can support and help you.

"I didn't really understand that my girlfriend was abusive. My friends would tell me that she was. It was my first relationship and I couldn't even see that. I couldn't see that it was all about her and her needs. She would make me feel guilty if I didn't do what she wanted, and she would get violent and blame me for everything. I was fearful inside and my grades fell, and I had a hard time concentrating. It's like I wasn't me anymore. I didn't live. I just existed. I never thought violence happened in lesbian relationships. I am a strong person and I didn't see that or understand it until later. I thought violence happened to weak people until it happened to me." Shawna, aged 17.

Speaking Up

Speaking up about abuse is a powerful and scary thing. First, you have to recognize or identify abuse for what it is. It is not a boyfriend or girlfriend "losing their temper" or "showing that they care." Speaking up means disclosing or telling someone about your experience. It means saying, "my boyfriend/girlfriend hurts me." Telling someone safe about the abuse means you aren't alone anymore and can be the first step in getting help.

Who Can We Talk To?

OK, so you think you might be ready to talk to someone; but how do you decide who that will be? When thinking about the right person to talk to, it is important to think about who you trust and who is safe. A safe person is someone who will listen to you, accept what you are saying, and be supportive. If you don't want to tell someone close to you, you can call a help line. Help lines are staffed with people who understand dating violence and date rape. They are trained to listen and provide support. You can find help lines in the phonebook and on the Internet. If you are afraid someone will find out, make sure you delete the history cache on the computer you use.

A Friend

If someone you know tells you they are experiencing dating violence, there are ways you can help. Listen, be supportive, and believe them. You might say something like, "What's happening isn't your fault. I'm worried about you." Just letting your friend know that you care about them and that you hear what they are saying can be a huge relief for someone experiencing violence. It is important to be respectful of their decisions. We might want to say, "Just leave!" But the decision to break up is extremely difficult and needs to be your friend's call. You can give your friend information about resources that can help them. This problem isn't yours or theirs to solve alone. There are people out there who can listen, be supportive, and help make you and the people you care about safe.

The Police

If you are in immediate danger, if someone is hurting you, threatening to hurt or kill you, or if they are at your house and will not leave, call 911. The police may be able to give you protection when you really need it or keep you safe long enough to escape from being hurt. The police can also help by documenting the abuse you have experienced (they take pictures and talk to witnesses). They can also help you get in touch with groups that can help. Some people feel uneasy about police. You may have had bad experiences with them in the past, or might feel worried about whether or not they will believe you. If you don't want to talk to police alone, you can ask a friend or family member to help you.

Restraining Orders

A restraining order is sometimes called a protective order. This is when a judge says that it is illegal for an abuser to harm you, come near you, or contact you. A restraining order can't make your abuser change and can't guarantee your safety. It can make it against the law for someone to contact you, hurt you, or come near you. Laws about restraining orders are different for each state and province. If you are under 18 years old, an adult may need to help you get one. For more information, you can talk to your local police station. Teachers, doctors, and guidance counselors are some other examples of adults you may know that you could talk to about experiencing dating violence or sexual assault.

Warning Signs

Are you in an abusive relationship? Sometimes it is difficult to tell because the warning signs may be subtle and the control gradual or **incremental**. Things to watch out for:

Are you afraid to express your feelings and opinions freely because you feel you will be ridiculed or ignored?

Does your girlfriend, boyfriend, date, or friend scare you?

Does their personality change when they drink or take drugs?

Do they do things to intimidate you?

Are you afraid to leave them or break up with them because they say they cannot live without you?

Do they bad-mouth former girlfriends or boyfriends and blame them for failed relationships?

Do they criticize you in private or in front of others?

Do they accuse you of things, such as talking to other boys or girls? Or do they threaten to break up with you if you do talk to other people?

Do they believe in strict gender roles, and that men should be in control of things and women should obey and do what they are told?

Are you worried about upsetting them or making them angry?

Do you always apologize for their behavior and make excuses for them when they lose their temper or act inappropriately?

Fear should never be a part of a healthy relationship. If fear is taking over your life, think about asking for help by talking to someone.

Chapter 7
Coping Toolbox

Everyone deserves a relationship that is safe and free from violence. If you are being hurt in your relationship, you might want to think about things you can do to keep yourself safe. It's not possible to control your partner, but there are some things that you can do to make yourself more safe.

Staying Safe and Breaking Up

A safety plan is a guide that is tailored to your life and your needs. It's a specific set of steps to follow that can make you as safe as possible. You can make a safety plan on your own or with an adult you trust.

If you have been experiencing abuse in your relationship, breaking up can be scary and even dangerous. If you are concerned about your safety, you don't have to break up in person, you can do it over the phone. Let someone know that you are planning to break up with your partner. You do not have to explain your reasons for breaking up with someone more than once. It won't make them less upset.

Safety Plan

Violence can happen at home, work, school, or when you're out with friends. Write out a safety plan and keep it with you just in case. You can also give a copy to someone you trust.

Things I can do to stay safe at home:

- If I had to leave my house in a hurry, what would I need to take? Where can I keep those things so that they are all together? (For example, wallet, phone, keys)

Things I can do to stay safe at school:

- What is the safest way to get to and from school?

Things I can do to stay safe when I'm with friends:

- Tell someone I trust where I'm going and who I will be with.

- Try double-dating with a friend so I don't have to be alone with a date.

Things I can do to stay safe emotionally:

- What clubs or groups can I join that interest me?

- What things can I do that I enjoy? (Some example are: dancing, riding bikes, listening to music)

Contact Numbers:

If I am feeling unsafe, or if I need support, who can I call?

In U.S.A.: 1-866-331-9474
(National Teen Dating Abuse Helpline)

In Canada: 1-800-668-6868
(Kids Help Phone)

Hot Topics
Q&A

Q: I sometimes say hurtful things to my partner, but I'm just teasing. Am I being abusive?

A: People often say hurtful things to one another. Saying mean things to put someone down, make them feel bad about themselves, control them, or humiliate them is abusive behavior. How might your words make your partner feel? Consider how you would like to be treated by your partner. If you need extra support, talk to someone you trust about how you might change your behavior.

Q: What if I am too afraid or ashamed to tell someone what is happening?

A: Sometimes abuse can creep up so slowly, we're not totally sure how it all started. What's worse, we feel ashamed and sad that the person we care about can hurt us. Dating violence is never your fault, and everyone has the right to a safe relationship. It can be very scary to think about talking to someone about dating violence, and it might take time to get comfortable with the idea. Talking to someone about what you're going through can help you to feel less alone and might make you feel better.

Q: I'm gay and my boyfriend assaulted me, but I haven't told anyone because I am not ready to let them know I am gay. Where can I go for help?

A: Dating abuse and date rape can occur between any two people in a dating relationship, including two men. If you are experiencing violence in your relationship, it is important to remember that you don't need to be alone. There are help lines you can call specifically for LGBTQ (Lesbian, Gay, Bisexual, Transgendered, Questioning) youth, staffed by people who understand what you are going through and are there to help. Try 1-800-246-PRIDE (1-800-246-7743) the GLBT National Youth Talkline, or www.gmdvp.org (Gay Men's Domestic Violence Project).

Q: My boyfriend hit me last month. It only happened once and he never hit me again. Can it be a one-time thing?

A: When someone has been violent once, they may use violence again. Often the violence can get worse or happen more often over time. Every relationship is different, and there can be long stretches where you don't get hurt at all. You deserve and have the right to a relationship that is safe and free from violence.

Q: I think I want to break up with my boyfriend, but I'm scared of what he might do. What should I say?

A: Tell your boyfriend that you do not want to date him anymore. You do not have to give your boyfriend a reason, and if you do, you do not need to explain it to him more than once. Make sure you tell someone you trust if you are frightened. They can help you make a safety plan to follow after the breakup.

Other Resources

There is a lot of information on dating violence and date rape, but you have to know where to look. Check your school or municipal library for books. You can also check the Internet for Web sites and hot lines. Here are some trustworthy resources to start with. The Web sites will contain useful information no matter which country you live in, but telephone numbers and referral services will be country-specific.

Helpful sites on dating violence and abuse:

www.thesafespace.org
www.breakthecycle.org
These two sites offer information on how to stay safe,
speak out, and break the cycle of violence.

In the United States

National Teen Dating Abuse Helpline
www.loveisrespect.org
1-866-331-9474
This is a 24-hour national hotline that supports teens (and parents) who are experiencing dating violence. You can call from anywhere in the U.S. toll free or log on to their Web site to receive information or assistance. This service is **confidential**.

The National Domestic Violence Hotline
www.ndvh.org
1-800-799-SAFE (7233)
This 24-hour national service assists with safety-planning and can

provide information and referrals to local community agencies. The service is available in English and Spanish, and it can also access interpreter services for over 100 languages.

National Hopeline Network
www.hopeline.com
1-800-SUICIDE (784-2433)
This is a 24-hour crisis line for teens who are thinking about suicide or who are experiencing violence. This is a national hotline, and callers are automatically routed to their community's local crisis service.

GLBT National Youth Talkline
1-800-246-PRIDE (1-800-246-7743)
This hotline offers telephone peer counseling to gay, lesbian, bisexual, and transgendered youth, Monday to Friday from 5-9 p.m. (Pacific Time).

Rape, Abuse & Incest National Network (RAINN)
www.rainn.org
1-800-656-HOPE (4673)
RAINN offers free, confidential, secure service that provides help for survivors of rape, abuse, and incest.

Gay Men's Domestic Violence Project
www.gmdvp.org
A non-profit organization dedicated to supporting male survivors of dating abuse in same-sex relationships.

In Canada
Kids Help Phone
1-800-668-6868
www.kidshelpphone.ca
This is a Canadian-only hotline, but the Web site will be useful to all pre-teens and teens. Professional counselors can answer any questions and give you referrals to services in your area.

Glossary

anxious A feeling of worry or nervousness

aroused Sexually excited

coercion To persuade someone to do something using force or threats

compromises Agreeing to make changes that are acceptable to all involved

confidential Something that is kept private or secret

forum A place where ideas and views can be exchanged

gender roles The cultural and social roles assigned to males and females in society

harrassed Subject to aggressive pressure, often with intimidation and threats

heterosexual A person sexually attracted to people of the opposite sex

humiliated To make someone feel ashamed by attacking their self-respect

incremental Small changes that happen slowly

inferior Lower in rank or status

intimate Familiar or close

intimidation To frighten someone in order to make them do what you want

manipulation To control or influence cleverly and unfairly

normalizes To make something seem normal

ogle To stare in a sexual manner

passive Allowing what happens, or what others do, to happen without resistance

perspective A view

psychologist An expert in the scientific study of the mind and human behavior

questioning Someone who is questioning or doubting their sexuality

reprisals An act of retaliation or an attack

sexual orientation Whether a person's sexual attraction is toward members of the opposite, same, or both sexes

social status A person's rank or standing in society

transgendered Feeling like you belong to a gender other than your biological one, or the one you were born with

traumatic Emotionally distressing, or extremely painful

verbal Through words

Index